101 Things To Do With A Slow Cooker

BY
STEPHANIE ASHCRAFT
AND JANET EYRING

Gibbs Smith, Publisher
Salt Lake City

First Edition
12 11 10   40 39 38 37

Published by
Gibbs Smith, Publisher
P.O. Box 667
Layton, Utah 84041

Orders: (1-800) 748-5439
www.gibbs-smith.com

Edited by Suzanne Gibbs Taylor
Designed and produced by Kurt Wahlner
Printed and bound in China

Library of Congress Cataloging-in-Publication Data

Ashcraft, Stephanie.
   101 things to do with a slow cooker / Stephanie Ashcraft and Janet
Eyring.--1st ed.
      p. cm.
   ISBN 1-58685-317-1
   1. Electric cookery, Slow. 2. Casserole cookery. I. Eyring, Janet.
II. Title.
TX827.A82 2003
641.5'884--dc21

                                        2003004842

101 Things To Do With A Slow Cooker

DEDICATION

Thank you to all the
people—especially our fami-
lies—who encouraged us to per-
severe and follow our dreams.

CONTENTS

Chicken

Chicken and Potatoes 68 • Chicken and Rice Casserole 69 • Scalloped Chicken 70 •
Whole Cranberry Chicken 71 • Mama's Italian Chicken 72 •
Favorite Barbecue Chicken 73 • Cheesy Chicken Noodles 74 •
Tater-Tot Casserole 75 • Hawaiian Chicken 76 • Easy Chicken Bake 77 •
Sunday Chicken 78 • Pineapple Chicken 79 • Lemonade Chicken 80 •
Sweet-and-Sour Chicken 81 • Hawaiian Haystacks 82 • Creamy Italian Chicken 83
• Italian Chicken with Mushrooms 84 • Creamy Chicken Soft Tacos 85 •
Orange Chicken 86 • Chicken Teriyaki 87 • Chicken Cacciatore 88 •
Chicken in a Bag 89 • Chicken Fajitas 90 • Chicken Parmesan 91 •
Almond Chicken 92 • Chicken Enchiladas 93 •
Cooked Chicken for Entrees, Soups, and Stews 94

Pork

Savory Pork Roast 97 • Cranberry Pork Roast 98 • Barbecued Pork Chops 99 •
Italian Pork Chops 100 • Sweet-and-Sour Pork 101 • Polynesian Pork Chops 102 •
Pork Chops and Mushrooms 103 • Pork Chop Casserole 104 • Ehlers' Pork Ribs 105
• Barbecue Pork Sandwiches 106 • Shredded Pork Burritos 107 •
Pork Sausage Casserole 108 • Ham and Potatoes 109 • Red Potatoes with Ham 110

•

Holiday Ham 111 • Shredded Ham Sandwiches 112

Desserts

Carrot Cake 115 • Caramel Rolls 116 • Triple Rich Chocolate Cake 117 •
Sugar and Spice Cake 118 • Cherry Biscuit Cobbler 119 •
Easy Granola Apple Crisp 120 • Cherry Jubilee 121 • Lemon Custard Cake 122 •
Pineapple Upside-Down Cake 123 • Chocolate Custard Cake 124

HELPFUL HINTS

1. To make clean-up easier, spray the inside of slow cooker with non-stick cooking spray before adding ingredients.

2. To test the cooking temperature of a slow cooker, fill it $3/4$ full of water, cover, and turn on high heat for 4 hours. With an instant heat thermometer, test water temperature immediately after lid is removed. Temperature should be at least 180 degrees. If the temperature is lower, we recommend replacing the slow cooker. If it is higher, check all recipes for doneness after 3 hours of cooking time.

3. As a general rule, lifting the lid off the slow cooker lengthens the cooking time by 30 minutes to an hour.

4. Stirring is generally not necessary until time to serve.

5. Your slow cooker should be at least $1/2$ full to ensure proper cooking.

6. Recipes that contain raw poultry or beef should cook a minimum of 3 hours on high heat. Combinations of raw meat and fresh vegetables should cook at least 4 hours on high heat.

7. Adapting favorite oven recipes to a slow cooker:

Conventional Oven *Baking Time*	Slow Cooker *High Cooking Time*	Slow Cooker *Low Cooking Time*
15–30 mins.	1 $1/2$–2 hours	4–6 hours
35–40 mins.	3–4 hours	6–10 hours
50 mins.–3 hours	4–6 hours	8–18 hours

8. One hour on high heat is equal to 2 $1/2$ hours on low heat. (High heat= 275-300 degrees; low heat=200 degrees. Heat varies from brand to brand.)

9. If your stoneware is removable, never place it on a stovetop burner.

10. At clean-up, cool the stoneware liner somewhat before adding water; this will prevent cracking.

11. Ground beef should be browned and drained before adding to slow cooker.

12. Fresh milk, cream, sour cream, and cream cheese should be added during the last hour of cooking to prevent curdling. Evaporated milk does not curdle and can be substituted for fresh milk in most recipes.

13. Long-grain converted rice is recommended for rice dishes.

14. Root vegetables (onions, carrots, potatoes, turnips) take longer to cook than meat. Place vegetables on bottom and around sides of slow cooker so they get the most direct heat.

15. Tough, inexpensive meat cuts work well. The moist, gentle heat slowly tenderizes these cuts as they cook.

16. Don't add more liquid than a recipe calls for, as liquid is retained.

17. If there's too much liquid at the end of cooking time and you want to thicken it, stir in some instant mashed potato flakes, instant tapioca, flour, or cornstarch.

18. If you start with a frozen cut of meat, add 2 hours to your cooking time on high heat or 4–6 hours on low heat.

19. For recipes that call for minced garlic, prepared jarred garlic may be substituted.

20. Fresh chopped onion can be used in place of dried minced onion. One medium fresh onion equals $1/2$ cup dried.

21. Recipes can be assembled and stored in the refrigerator the night before (unless they call for uncooked pasta). In the morning, place cold stoneware in cold electrical base. DO NOT PREHEAT ELECTRICAL BASE. Once stoneware is in place, turn to preferred heat setting.

22. To remove scratches from stoneware, use Bon Ami or vinegar and baking soda. Baking soda also works well to clean the electrical base. DO NOT SUBMERGE ELECTRICAL BASE IN WATER.

Happy slow cooking!

BEVERAGES

PARTY HOT CHOCOLATE

4 to 5 cups	**nonfat dry milk**
$3/4$ to 1 cup	**sugar**
$1/2$ to $3/4$ cup	**baking cocoa**
2 teaspoons	**vanilla**
11 cups	**water**

Combine all ingredients in 4 $1/2$ to 6-quart slow cooker. Cover and cook on low heat 3–4 hours, stirring occasionally. *Makes 10–15 servings.*

Serve with whipped cream sprinkled with mini chocolate chips or white chocolate chips.

MALLOW-MINT HOT CHOCOLATE

4 to 5 cups	**nonfat dry milk**
$^1/_2$ to $^3/_4$ cup	**baking cocoa**
$^3/_4$ to I cup	**sugar**
II cups	**water**
2 teaspoons	**mint extract**
	marshmallows

Combine all ingredients in 4 $^1/_2$ to 6-quart slow cooker. Cover and cook on low heat 3–4 hours, stirring occasionally. *Makes 10–15 servings.*

Serve with mint chocolate chips or a small peppermint candy cane.

ALMOND HOT CHOCOLATE

4 to 5 cups	**nonfat dry milk**
$^1/_2$ to $^3/_4$ cup	**baking cocoa**
$^3/_4$ cup	**sugar**
11 cups	**water**
2 teaspoons	**almond extract**

Combine all ingredients in 4 $^1/_2$ to 6-quart slow cooker. Cover and cook on low heat 3–4 hours. Stir occasionally. *Makes 10–15 servings.*

Top each cup of chocolate with whipped cream and a dash of cinnamon.

HOT CRANBERRY PUNCH

4 cups	unsweetened pineapple juice
4 cups	cranberry juice cocktail
1/2 cup	packed brown sugar
1 cup	water
1/2 teaspoon	ground cloves
1	cinnamon stick

Combine all ingredients in 3 1/2 to 5-quart slow cooker. Cover and cook on low heat 4–10 hours. When ready to serve, remove cinnamon stick. *Makes 8–10 servings.*

HOLIDAY WASSAIL

3 sticks	**cinnamon** (3-inch pieces)
2 teaspoons	**ground cloves**
8 cups	**water**
$3/4$ cup	**frozen cranberry juice cocktail concentrate**
$3/4$ cup frozen	**raspberry juice concentrate**
$3/4$ cup frozen	**apple juice concentrate**
$1/2$ cup	**sugar**
$1/3$ cup	**lemon juice**
	orange slices, optional

In a in 3 $1/2$ to 5-quart slow cooker, combine all ingredients except orange slices. Cover and cook on high heat for 2−3 hours or on low heat for 5−6 hours. Float orange slices in slow cooker during the last hour of cooking. *Makes 12−15 servings.*

HOT SPICED CHERRY CIDER

3 1/2 quarts	**apple cider**
2	**cinnamon sticks**
1 package (3 ounces)	**cherry-flavored gelatin**

In a 4 to 6-quart slow cooker, add cinnamon sticks to apple cider and stir. Heat on high 3 hours. Stir in gelatin. Leave on high heat 1 more hour, until gelatin dissolves, stirring once or twice. Turn on low heat to keep warm. Remove cinnamon sticks before serving. *Makes 10–15 servings.*

For a more intense cherry flavor, add an additional package of gelatin.

Dips and Fondues

MILD CHILI-CHEESE DIP

2 cans (15 ounces each)   **chili,** with or without beans
1 pound   **mild Velveeta cheese,** cubed

Combine chili and cheese in greased 3 $1/2$ to 4-quart slow cooker and cook on low heat 1 $1/2$ to 3 hours, stirring every 30 minutes, until cheese is melted. *Makes 10–15 servings.*

Serve with tortilla chips or celery sticks, or as a condiment for fries or potato wedges.

BODACIOUS BEAN DIP

I can (20 ounces)	**refried beans**
1/2 cup	**green onion,** chopped
1/4 teaspoon	**salt**
I 1/2 tablespoons	**taco seasoning**
I cup	**cheddar cheese,** shredded

Combine all ingredients except cheese in greased 2 to 3 1/2-quart slow cooker. Cover and cook on high heat 30 minutes and then on low heat for an additional 30 minutes, or on low heat 2–3 hours. Add cheddar cheese the last hour on low heat. *Makes 4–8 servings.*

Serve with tortilla chips or wrapped in a warm flour tortilla.

PIZZA FONDUE

1 jar (26 to 28 ounces)	**spaghetti sauce with meat**
2 teaspoons	**Italian seasoning**
1 tablespoon	**cornstarch** or **instant tapioca**
1/2 cup	**sliced pepperoni**
1 cup	**mozzarella cheese,** grated

Combine all ingredients except mozzarella cheese in greased 2 to 3 1/2-quart slow cooker. Cover and cook on low heat for 2–3 hours. Add cheese the last hour of cooking. *Makes 8–10 servings.*

Dip bread sticks, pita bread, or chunks of crusty Italian bread.

CHEESE FONDUE

2 cans (10 $^3/_4$ ounces each)	**cheese soup**
1 tablespoon	**Worcestershire sauce**
1 teaspoon	**lemon juice**
2 tablespoons	**dried chopped chives,** optional
2 cups	**sharp cheddar cheese,** grated

Combine soup, Worcestershire sauce, lemon juice, and chives in greased 2 to 3 $^1/_2$-quart slow cooker. Cover and cook on low heat for 2–2 $^1/_2$ hours. Add cheese the last hour of cooking, stirring to combine. *Makes 8–12 servings.*

Dip crudités (celery sticks, cauliflower or broccoli florets, blanched asparagus) in warm fondue. Leftover fondue can be reheated as a sauce for white fish, Brussels sprouts, or baked potatoes.

CHOCOLATE FONDUE

2 cups **milk chocolate chips**
²/₃ cup **half-and-half**

Stir chocolate chips and half-and-half together in greased 1 to 2-quart slow cooker. Cover and cook on low heat for 1 hour. Stir halfway through cooking time and again when fondue is finished. *Makes 6–8 servings.*

Dip fresh strawberries or chunks of angel food cake.

CARAMEL FONDUE

  $^1/_2$ cup **butter**
  $^1/_2$ cup **light corn syrup**
   I cup **brown sugar**
   I can **sweetened condensed milk**

In a saucepan, mix together all ingredients and bring to boil. Transfer
to greased I to 2 $^1/_2$-quart slow cooker and set on low heat to serve.
Makes 6–8 servings.

Dip apple slices or chunks of angel food cake. Or spoon over apple-
spice cake.

PEANUT BUTTER FONDUE

¹/₂ cup	**butter**
¹/₂ cup	**light corn syrup**
I cup	**brown sugar**
I can	**sweetened condensed milk**
¹/₂ cup	**peanut butter**

In a saucepan, mix together all ingredients and bring to boil. Transfer to greased I to 2 ¹/₂-quart slow cooker and set on low heat to serve. *Makes 8–10 servings.*

Serve with slices of cake, apples, or bananas for dipping.

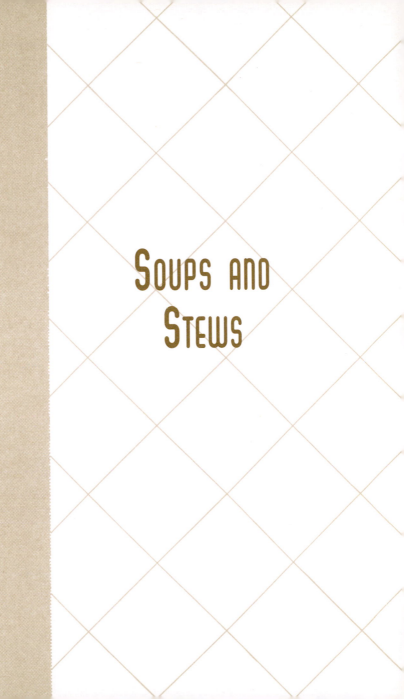

SOUPS AND STEWS

HEARTY VEGETABLE SOUP

I pound	**round steak,** cut in I-inch cubes
I can (14 ¹/₂ ounces)	**diced tomatoes**
2 cups	**water**
2	**new or white potatoes,** cubed
³/₄ cup	**dried minced onion**
15	**baby carrots,** cut in thirds
I can (15 ounces)	**green beans**
I can (15 ounces)	**whole kernel corn**
3 cubes	**beef bouillon**
¹/₂ teaspoon	**dried basil**
¹/₂ teaspoon	**dried oregano**
I teaspoon	**salt**
¹/₄ teaspoon	**pepper**

Combine all ingredients in greased 3 ¹/₂ to 5-quart slow cooker. Cover and cook on high heat 3–4 hours or on low heat 6–8 hours. *Makes 4–6 servings.*

Serve with corn bread or bran muffins.

QUICK STEW

2 pounds	**stewing beef,** cubed
15	**baby carrots,** halved
$^1/_2$ cup	**dried minced onion**
3 large	**potatoes,** cubed
I can (10 $^3/_4$ ounces)	**tomato soup**
I soup can	**water**
I teaspoon	**salt**
2 tablespoons	**vinegar**
	pepper, to taste

Combine all ingredients in greased 3 $^1/_2$ to 5-quart slow cooker. Cover and cook on high heat 5–6 hours or on low heat 10–12 hours. *Makes 4–6 servings.*

Serve in bread bowls. the liquid seems too thin, thicken it by stirring in small amounts of dehydrated potato until it reaches the desired thickness.

ZESTY MINESTRONE

3 cups	**water**
1 1/2 pounds	**stewing beef,** cut into 1-inch pieces and browned
1/4 cup	**dried minced onion**
20	**baby carrots,** cut in thirds
1 can (14 1/2 ounces)	**diced tomatoes**
1 teaspoon	**salt**
1 tablespoon	**dried basil**
1/2 cup	**dried vermicelli**
1 1/2 tablespoons	**dried oregano**
1 package (10 ounces)	**frozen mixed vegetables**
1/4 cup	**grated Parmesan cheese**

Combine all ingredients except frozen vegetables and cheese in greased 3 1/2 to 5-quart slow cooker. Cover and cook on high heat 3–4 hours or on low heat 6–8 hours. One hour before serving, add frozen vegetables. Cover and cook an additional hour. Top individual servings with Parmesan cheese. *Makes 4–6 servings.*

Serve with crusty bread and herbed cream cheese spread.

BURTON'S MINESTRONE

1/2 to 1 pound	**ground beef,** browned and drained
2 cans (10 3/4 ounces)	**minestrone soup**
2 cups	**water**
2 cans (15 ounces)	**pork and beans**
1 cup	**shredded carrots**
1/2 cup	**dried minced onion** or
1	**large fresh onion,** chopped
1 1/2 tablespoons	**Worcestershire sauce**
1/2 teaspoon	**oregano**

Combine all ingredients in greased 4 to 6-quart slow cooker. Cover and cook on low heat 3–5 hours. *Makes 4–6 servings.*

Serve with warm bread sticks.

COWBOY SOUP

1 pound	**ground beef,** browned and drained
1 can (14 $^{1}/_{2}$ ounces)	**crushed tomatoes**
1 can (14 $^{1}/_{2}$ ounces)	**diced tomatoes with green chilies***
1 can (15 ounces)	**whole kernel corn,** drained
$^{1}/_{2}$ cup	**dried minced onion**
1 box (6.8 ounces)	**Spanish rice**

Combine all ingredients in greased 4 $^{1}/_{2}$ to 6-quart slow cooker. Cover and cook on low heat 4–5 hours. Do not overcook. *Makes 4–6 servings.*

Top with grated cheese and sour cream, if desired. Serve with tortilla chips.

*For a spicier version, us diced tomatoes with jalapeños.

ALPHABET SOUP

$^1/_2$ pound	**stewing meat,** cubed
I can (14 $^1/_2$ ounces)	**stewed tomatoes**
I can (8 ounces)	**tomato sauce**
I cup	**water**
I envelope	**dry onion soup mix**
I package (10 ounces)	**frozen mixed vegetables,** partially thawed
$^1/_2$ cup	**uncooked alphabet pasta**

Combine meat, tomatoes, tomato sauce, water, and soup mix in greased 3 $^1/_2$ to 5-quart slow cooker. Cover and cook on low heat 6–8 hours. A half hour before serving, stir in vegetables and noodles. Cover and cook on high heat for 30 minutes. Add more water if mixture is too dry or too thick. *Makes 4–6 servings.*

Serve with oyster soup crackers.

SPICY TOMATO BEEF SOUP

I pound	**ground beef,** browned and drained
$^1/_2$ cup	**dried minced onions**
I jar (26 ounces)	**spaghetti sauce**
3 $^1/_2$ cups	**water**
I can (14 $^1/_2$ ounces)	**diced tomatoes with green chilies**
I cup	**celery,** sliced
I teaspoon	**beef bouillon granules** or
I cube	**beef bouillon**
I teaspoon	**pepper**

Combine all ingredients in greased 3 $^1/_2$ to 5-quart slow cooker. Cover and cook on high heat 3–4 hours or on low heat 5–6 hours. *Makes 4–6 servings.*

Serve with pita pockets stuffed with spring salad mix and rings of red onion and green pepper.

SANTA FE CHEESE SOUP

1 pound	**Velveeta cheese,** cubed
1 pound	**ground beef,** browned and drained
1 can (15 1/4 ounces)	**whole kernel corn,** with liquid
1 can (15 ounces)	**kidney beans,** with liquid
1 can (14 1/2 ounces)	**diced tomatoes with green chilies**
1 can (14 1/2 ounces)	**stewed tomatoes,** diced, with liquid
1 envelope	**taco seasoning mix**

Combine all ingredients in greased 4 1/2 to 6-quart slow cooker. Cover and cook on high heat 3 hours or on low heat 4–5 hours. *Makes 6–8 servings.*

Serve with corn chips.

SALSA FEVER SOUP

    3 cups   **Ortega Salsa Prima Mexican-Style Salsa**
    6 cups   **beef broth**
    $^1/_2$ cup   **long-grain white rice,** uncooked

Combine all ingredients in greased 4 to 6-quart slow cooker. Cover and cook on low heat 4–6 hours, or until rice is done. Do not overcook. *Makes 6–8 servings.*

Serve with warm flour tortillas and a side salad of cucumber, onion, and tomato.

SIMPLE CHILI

2 pounds	**ground beef,** browned and drained
1/2 cup	**dried minced onion** or
1	**large onion,** chopped
1 large can (28 ounces)	**diced tomatoes**
2 cans (8 ounces each)	**tomato purée**
1 can (16 ounces)	**kidney beans,** with liquid
1 can (4 ounces)	**diced green chilies**
1 cup	**water**
1 teaspoon	**minced garlic**
2 tablespoons	**chili powder**
2 teaspoons	**salt**
1 teaspoon	**pepper**
	bread bowls

Combine all ingredients in greased 4 1/2 to 6-quart slow cooker. Cover and cook on high heat 2–3 hours or on low heat 4–6 hours. Serve in bread bowls. *Makes 6–8 servings.*

Garnish with sour cream, chives, and grated cheddar cheese.

CHICKEN NOODLE SOUP

5 cups	**hot water**
2 tablespoons	**instant chicken bouillon granules**
1 large can (46 ounces)	**chicken broth**
2 cups	**cooked chicken**
1 teaspoon	**salt**
15	**baby carrots,** cut in thirds
3 cups	**egg noodles,** uncooked

Combine all ingredients except egg noodles in greased 3 $1/2$ to 5-quart slow cooker. Cover and cook on low heat 4–6 hours. Thirty minutes before serving, stir in egg noodles. Cover and cook on low heat for an additional 30 minutes. Do not overcook. *Makes 4–6 servings.*

Serve with a salad of steamed fresh green beans, red onion, crumbled bacon, and parmesan cheese.

TORTILLA SOUP

4	**boneless, skinless chicken breasts,** cooked and shredded
1/2 teaspoon	**minced garlic**
2 cans (14 ounces each)	**chicken broth**
2 cans (14 ounces each)	**stewed tomatoes,** chopped
1 cup	**medium salsa**
2 tablespoons	**dried cilantro**
1 tablespoon	**ground cumin**
3–4	**flour or corn tortillas,** cut into 1/2-inch strips
	cheese, grated

Combine all ingredients in greased 4 1/2 to 6-quart slow cooker. Cover and cook on high heat 4–6 hours or on low heat 8–10 hours. Ladle hot soup into individual serving bowls over strips of flour tortilla and grated Monterey Jack or cheddar cheese. *Makes 6–8 servings.*

Serve tortilla chips with guacamole and sour cream.

TURKEY AND RICE SOUP

I	**small onion,** chopped
I cup	**celery,** diced
2 to 3 cups	**cooked turkey,** diced
I cup	**converted white rice,** uncooked
4 cups	**water**
I jar (12 ounces)	**turkey gravy**
1/2 teaspoon	**salt**
1/4 teaspoon	**pepper**

Combine all ingredients in greased 3 1/2 to 5-quart slow cooker. Cover and cook on low heat 5–7 hours, or until rice is done. Do not overcook. *Makes 4–6 servings.*

Serve with honey wheat rolls and fresh fruit.

BROCCOLI-CHEESE SOUP

2 packages (16 ounces each)	**frozen chopped broccoli**
2 cans (10 $^3/_4$ ounces each)	**cheddar cheese soup**
2 cans (12 ounces each)	**evaporated milk**
$^1/_4$ cup	**dried minced onion**
$^1/_2$ teaspoon	**salt**
$^1/_4$ teaspoon	**pepper**

Combine all ingredients except bacon in greased 4 to 6-quart slow cooker. Cover and cook on high heat 2–3 hours or on low heat 4–5 hours. *Makes 4–6 servings.*

Spoon over baked potato or simply garnish with bacon.

FOUR-HOUR STEW

2 pounds	**stew meat,** cubed
2 cups	**new or white potatoes,** quartered
20	**baby carrots,** cut in thirds
I can (10 $^3/_4$ ounces)	**cream of celery soup**
I can (10 $^3/_4$ ounces)	**cream of mushroom soup**
I soup can	**water**
I envelope	**dry onion soup mix**

Combine all ingredients in greased 3 $^1/_2$ to 5-quart slow cooker. Cover and cook on high heat 4 hours or on low heat 6–8 hours. *Makes 4–6 servings.*

Serve with biscuits fresh from the oven.

EASY TACO SOUP

I can (15 ounces)	**chili with beans and meat**
I can (15 ounces)	**whole kernel corn,** with liquid
I can (14 1/2 ounces)	**diced tomatoes,** with liquid
I can (8 ounces)	**tomato sauce**
I can (15 ounces)	**black beans,** with liquid
I 1/2 to 3 tablespoons	**dry taco seasoning mix**

Combine all ingredients in greased 3 1/2 to 4 1/2-quart slow cooker. Cover and cook on low heat 6–8 hours. *Makes 4–6 servings.*

Serve with quesadillas.

VEGETABLE CHEESE SOUP

1 can (15 ounces)	**cream-style corn**
3 to 4	**new or red potatoes,** quartered
1/2 cup	**shredded** or **julienne carrots**
1/2 cup	**chopped onion** or
1/4 cup	**dried minced onion**
1/4 teaspoon	**pepper**
2 cans (14 1/4 ounces each)	**vegetable broth**
1 1/2 cups	**shredded cheddar cheese**

Combine all ingredients except cheese in greased 3 1/2 to 5-quart slow cooker. Cover and cook on high heat 4–5 hours or on low heat 6–8 hours. Just before serving, stir in cheese until melted. *Makes 4–6 servings.*

Serve with a salad of leaf lettuce, thawed green peas, sliced green onion and crumbled bacon.

CHICKEN AND WILD RICE SOUP

I can (10 ³/₄ ounces)	**condensed cream of chicken soup**
2 cups	**cooked chicken,** chopped
I cup	**carrots,** shredded
I cup	**celery,** diced
2 packages (4 ounces each)	**long grain and wild rice mix,** with seasoning packets
5 cups	**chicken broth**
5 cups	**water**

Combine all ingredients in a greased 4 ¹/₂ to 6-quart slow cooker. Cover and cook on low heat 4–6 hours, or until rice is done. Do not overcook. *Makes 6–8 servings.*

Serve with zucchini bread or applesauce muffins.

BEEF

SUNDAY ROAST

3 to 4 pound	**rump roast**
1 pound bag	**baby carrots**
1 cup	**chopped onion,** or
1/2 cup	**dried minced onion**
8 to 10	**red potatoes,** quartered
1 envelope	**dry onion soup mix**
1 cup	**water**

Place carrots, onion, and potatoes in bottom of greased 4 to 5-quart slow cooker. Place meat on top of vegetables. Dissolve soup mix in water and pour over meat. Cover and cook on low heat 8–10 hours. If using a frozen roast, cook on low heat an additional 2–4 hours. *Makes 6–8 servings.*

Serve with a green bean-and-mushroom medley.

COLA ROAST

3 pound	**beef roast**
1 envelope	**dry onion soup mix**
2 cans (12 ounces each)	**cola***

Place roast in greased 4 to 5-quart slow cooker. Sprinkle with soup mix. Pour soda over all. Cover and cook on low heat 7–8 hours. *Makes 4–6 servings.*

Serve with scalloped potatoes.

*Diet soda cannot be substituted.

SOUTH-OF-THE-BORDER POT ROAST

3 pound **chuck roast**
1 envelope **taco seasoning**
$^1/_2$ cup **water**

Place meat in greased 3 $^1/_2$ to 5-quart slow cooker. Combine taco seasoning and water and pour over meat. Cover and cook on low heat 10–12 hours. *Makes 4–6 servings.*

Serve with Spanish rice plus steamed zucchini and summer squash.

EASY SWISS STEAK

1 1/2 pounds	**round steak,** cut into serving-size pieces
1 pound	**baby carrots**
1 envelope	**dry onion soup mix**
1 can (8 ounces)	**tomato sauce**
1/2 cup	**water**

Place carrots in bottom of greased 3 1/2 to 5-quart slow cooker. Top with steak. Combine soup mix, tomato sauce, and water. Pour over other ingredients. Cover and cook on low heat 8–10 hours. To serve the steak, ladle over plain or garlic mashed potatoes. *Makes 4–6 servings.*

Serve with a side of cucumber and onion marinated in vinegar.

BEEF AND MUSHROOMS

3 pounds	**stew meat,** cubed
I can (10 $^3/_4$ ounces)	**cream of mushroom soup**
2 cans (4 ounces each)	**mushrooms,** with liquid
$^1/_2$ cup	**apple juice**
I envelope	**dry onion soup mix**

Combine all ingredients in greased 3 $^1/_2$ to 5-quart slow cooker. Cover and cook on low heat 10 hours. *Makes 4–6 servings.*

Serve in bowls, ladled over rice. Accompany with a sauté of fresh vegetables.

SIMPLE BEEF STROGANOFF

I pound **stew meat,** cubed
$^1/_2$ cup **dried minced onion**
I can (10 $^3/_4$ ounces) **cream of mushroom soup**
I (4 ounce) **can mushrooms,** drained
$^1/_4$ teaspoon **garlic salt**
I cup **sour cream***

Combine all ingredients except sour cream in greased 3 $^1/_2$ to 5-quart slow cooker. Cover and cook on low heat 6–8 hours. Add sour cream the last hour of cooking. *Makes 4–6 servings.*

Spoon over hot noodles. Add a salad of red cabbage and apricots tossed with balsamic vinegar and oil.

*Can substitute I package (8 ounces) cream cheese for sour cream.

FRENCH DIP SANDWICHES

2 to 3 pound **rump roast**
2 cans (14 $^1/_2$ ounces each) **beef consommé**
4–6 **hoagie buns**

Place roast in greased 3 $^1/_2$ to 5-quart slow cooker. Pour consommé over the top of roast. Cover and cook on low heat 8–10 hours or on high heat 5–7 hours. Remove roast and save extra juice. With a fork, break apart meat and serve on hoagies. Use excess juice for dipping sandwiches. *Makes 4–6 servings.*

Serve with crispy cole slaw.

LASAGNA

12	**lasagna noodles,** uncooked
I pound	**ground beef,** browned and drained
I teaspoon	**Italian seasoning**
I jar (28 ounces)	**spaghetti sauce**
$1/4$ cup	**water**
I carton (16 ounces)	**cottage cheese**
2 cups	**mozzarella cheese,** grated

Break noodles in half. Place half of the noodles in bottom of greased 4-quart slow cooker. Stir Italian seasoning into meat and spread half over the noodles already in slow cooker. Then layer half of the sauce and water, half of cottage cheese, and half of mozzarella cheese over beef. Repeat layers. Cover and cook on low heat 4–5 hours. Do not cook more than 5 hours. *Makes 6–8 servings.*

Serve with Greek salad: greens, tomatoes, olives, and feta cheese.

BURRITOS

1 pound	**ground beef,** cooked and drained
2 cans (16 ounces each)	**refried beans**
1 envelope	**taco seasoning**
1 can (8 ounces)	**tomato sauce**
½ cup	**water**
	flour tortillas

Combine all ingredients except tortillas in greased 3 ½ to 5-quart slow cooker. Cover and cook on low heat 6–10 hours. Spread hot bean mixture on flour tortillas. Fill with favorite burrito toppings. Fold and enjoy. *Makes 4–6 servings.*

Burrito toppings might include tomatoes, whole kernel corn, green onions, cheese, guacamole, caramelized onion, and red or green salsa.

EASY FLANK STEAK

1 1/2 pounds	**flank steak,** cut to fit in slow cooker
1/3 cup	**water**
1 can (4 ounces)	**chopped green chilies**
2 tablespoons	**vinegar**
1 1/4 teaspoons	**chili powder**
1 teaspoon	**garlic powder**
1/2 teaspoon	**sugar**
1/2 teaspoon	**salt**
1/4 teaspoon	**pepper**

Place meat in greased 3 1/2 to 5-quart slow cooker. Combine other
ingredients and sprinkle over the top of meat. Cover and cook on low
heat 8–10 hours. *Makes 4–6 servings.*

Mix garlic-and-herb cream cheese into mashed potatoes.

SWEET-AND-SOUR BEEF

2 pounds	**stew meat,** cubed
1 bottle (10 ounces)	**sweet-and-sour sauce**
1 cup	**shredded carrots**
4–6 cups	**hot cooked rice**

Combine all ingredients in greased 2 to 3 $\frac{1}{2}$-quart slow cooker. Cover and cook on low heat 6–8 hours. Ladle over hot cooked rice. *Makes 4–6 servings.*

Serve with an oriental vegetable stir fry.

UNBELIEVABLY SIMPLE BRISKET

4 to 5 pounds	**fresh beef brisket**
I envelope	**dry onion soup mix**
I can (4 ounces)	**mushrooms,** with liquid

Trim all excess fat from meat. Combine soup mix with mushrooms and mushroom liquid. Place meat in greased 4 1/2 to 6-quart slow cooker, cutting to fit if necessary. Spread onion soup mixture over brisket, moistening well. Cover and cook on low heat for 10–14 hours. Remove meat and cut across the grain into thin slices. Serve with meat juices poured over top of slices. *Makes 6–8 servings.*

Serve with baked sweet potatoes sprinkled with cinnamon sugar.

FAMILY FAVORITE BRISKET

4 pounds	**fresh beef brisket**
I teaspoon	**salt**
2 teaspoons	**dry mustard**
2 teaspoons	**paprika**
$^1/_2$ to I teaspoon	**garlic powder**
	pepper, to taste

Trim all excess fat from meat. Combine seasonings until well blended; rub into brisket. Place meat in greased 4 to 6-quart slow cooker, with the side that had more fat on top, cutting to fit if necessary. Cover and cook on low heat for 10–12 hours. Remove meat from liquid and cut across grain into thin slices. *Makes 4–6 servings.*

Serve with your favorite potato salad and fresh veggies with dip.

TRI-TIP ROAST

3 to 4 pound	**Tri-Tip Roast**
I can (10 ³/₄ ounces)	**cream of celery soup**
I can (10 ³/₄ ounces)	**cream of mushroom soup**
I can (14 ounces)	**beef broth**
	salt and pepper, to taste

Salt and pepper the roast. Place in greased 3 ¹/₂ to 5-quart slow cooker. Mix soups and broth and pour over roast. Cook on high heat 4–6 hours or low heat 8–10 hours. *Makes 4–6 servings.*

Serve with popovers, boiled potatoes, or noodles.

SHEPHERD'S PIE

1 pound	**ground beef,** browned and drained
1 can (15 ounces)	**whole kernel corn,** drained
1 can (15 ounces)	**French cut green beans,** drained
2 cups	**instant mashed potatoes,** prepared
2 cups	**grated cheddar cheese**
1/2 teaspoon	**dried basil**

In a separate bowl, combine beef, corn, and beans. Pour mixture in the bottom of a greased 3 1/2 to 5-quart slow cooker. Spread mashed potatoes on top. Cover and cook on low heat 5–6 hours. The last hour of cooking, sprinkle cheese on top of potatoes. *Makes 4–6 servings.*

Serve with wheat rolls.

AUNT PATTY'S
ITALIAN BARBECUE

2 pounds	**frozen chuck roast**
I envelope	**dry Italian salad dressing mix**
I tablespoon	**minced garlic**
8–10	**hamburger buns**

Place meat in greased 3 $\frac{1}{2}$ to 4 $\frac{1}{2}$-quart slow cooker. Sprinkle dry seasoning mix and minced garlic over the top. Cover and cook on high heat 6–8 hours or on low heat 14–18 hours. Before serving, remove fat and shred meat with a fork or potato masher. Serve on warm hamburger buns. *Makes 8–10 servings.*

Serve with a pasta salad or a hot macaroni dish.

ONION MEATBALLS

2 packages (18 ounces each)	**frozen cooked meatballs**
1 jar (12 ounces)	**beef gravy**
1 envelope	**dry onion soup mix**

Combine all ingredients in greased 3 $1/2$ to 4-quart slow cooker. Cook on low heat 3–4 hours. *Makes 4–6 servings.*

Meatballs can be served on a platter with toothpicks as appetizers, or on toasted hoagies with provolone cheese as sandwiches.

BARBECUED MEATBALLS

2 packages (18 ounces each)	**frozen cooked meatballs***
1 bottle (16 ounces)	**barbecue sauce**
1/3 cup	**chopped onions**

Combine all ingredients in greased 3 1/2 to 4-quart slow cooker. Cook on low heat 3–4 hours. *Makes 4–6 servings.*

Meatballs can be served with toothpicks as appetizers, or on toasted hoagies with mozzarella cheese as sandwiches.

*Cocktail sausages could be substituted.

CHICKEN

CHICKEN AND POTATOES

¹/₂ cup	**margarine** or **butter,** melted
¹/₄ cup	**dried, minced onion**
I package (16 ounces)	**frozen hashed brown potatoes**
I can (8 ounces or larger)	**cooked chicken,** drained
I can (10 ³/₄ ounces)	**cream of mushroom soup**
I ¹/₂ cups	**milk**
I cup	**cheddar cheese,** grated
¹/₄ teaspoon	**black pepper**
I cup	**cheese cracker crumbs,** divided

In a large bowl, mix together all ingredients except half of the cracker crumbs. Transfer to a greased 3 ¹/₂ to 5-quart slow cooker. Top with remaining cracker crumbs. Cover and cook on high heat 3–4 hours or on low heat 6–8 hours. *Makes 4–6 servings.*

Serve with mixed-fruit ambrosia (slices of orange, grapefruit, banana, strawberry, and apple tossed with coconut).

CHICKEN AND RICE CASSEROLE

I can (10 3/4 ounces)	**cream of celery soup**
I can (4 ounces)	**sliced mushrooms,** with liquid
1/2 cup	**long-grain, converted white rice,** uncooked
2	**breasts of chicken,** cooked and cubed
I tablespoon	**dry onion soup mix**

Combine soup, mushrooms, and rice in greased 2 to 3 1/2-quart slow cooker. Place chicken on top of mixture and sprinkle with onion soup mix. Cover and cook on low heat 4–6 hours. *Makes 2–4 servings.*

Serve with Caesar salad.

SCALLOPED CHICKEN

1 box (5 ounces)	**scalloped potatoes,** including seasoning packet
1 can (8 ounces or larger)	**white meat chicken**
3 ³/₄ cups	**water**

Put potatoes in greased 2 ¹/₂ to 3 ¹/₂-quart slow cooker first, followed by seasoning packet and chicken. Pour water over all. Cover and cook on high heat 1 ¹/₂–2 hours or on low heat 4–5 hours. *Makes 4–6 servings.*

Serve with steamed asparagus sprinkled with parmesan cheese.

WHOLE CRANBERRY CHICKEN

3 to 4 pounds	**chicken pieces**
$^1/_4$ cup	**dried minced onion**
I can (16 ounces)	**whole berry cranberry sauce***
I cup	**barbecue sauce**
	salt and pepper, to taste

Combine all ingredients in greased 3 $^1/_4$ to 5-quart slow cooker. Cover and cook on high heat 4 hours or on low heat 6–8 hours. *Makes 4–6 servings.*

Serve with baked potatoes and a side of stuffing!

*Do not use jellied cranberry sauce as it adds too much liquid.

MAMA'S ITALIAN CHICKEN

4	**frozen chicken breast halves**
I envelope	**dry Italian salad dressing mix**
I can (14 ounces)	**chicken broth**

Place chicken in greased 3 $^1/_2$ to 4 $^1/_2$-quart slow cooker. Sprinkle with salad dressing mix. Pour chicken broth over the top. Cover and cook on high heat 4–5 hours or on low heat 8–10 hours. *Makes 4 servings.*

Serve on a nest of buttered noodles or creamy risotto.

FAVORITE BARBECUE CHICKEN

4 to 6 **boneless, skinless chicken breasts**
I bottle (16 ounces) **barbecue sauce**

Put chicken in greased 3 $\frac{1}{2}$ to 5-quart slow cooker. Pour favorite barbecue sauce over the top. Cook on high heat 4–6 hours or on low heat 8–10 hours. *Makes 4–6 servings.*

Leftovers can be shredded for sandwiches.

CHEESY CHICKEN NOODLES

6	**boneless, skinless chicken breasts**
2 cans (10 $^3/_4$ ounces each)	**broccoli cheese soup**
2 cups	**milk**
$^1/_2$ cup	**dried minced onion**
$^1/_2$ teaspoon	**dried basil**
	salt and pepper, to taste
	egg noodles

Place chicken in greased 4 $^1/_2$ to 6-quart slow cooker. Combine remaining ingredients and pour over chicken. Cover and cook on high heat 1 hour and then reduce to low heat and cook 5–6 hours. Serve over hot cooked noodles. *Makes 6 servings.*

Serve with tossed green salad or fresh veggies.

TATER-TOT CASSEROLE

I bag (32 ounces)	**frozen tater tots**
I can (8 ounces)	**chicken,** drained*
$^1/_2$ teaspoon	**salt**
$^1/_4$ teaspoon	**pepper**
I can (14 $^1/_2$ ounces)	**green beans,** drained
I can (10 $^3/_4$ ounces)	**cream of mushroom soup**
I tablespoon	**dried onions**
$^1/_2$ cup	**milk**
$^1/_2$ cup	**cheddar cheese,** grated

Pour bag of frozen tater tots on bottom of greased 4 $^1/_2$ to 6-quart slow cooker. In separate bowl, combine remaining ingredients except cheese and pour over potatoes. Cover and cook on high heat 3 hours or on low heat 4 $^1/_2$–5 hours. Half an hour before serving, sprinkle grated cheese over the top. *Makes 4–6 servings.*

Serve with apple slices and grapes.

*Tuna may be substituted.

HAWAIIAN CHICKEN

4 to 6	**boneless, skinless chicken breasts**
I can (8 ounces)	**crushed pineapple**
I bottle (16 ounces)	**barbecue sauce**
4 to 6 cups	**rice,** cooked

Place meat in greased 3 $^{1}/_{2}$ to 5-quart slow cooker. Combine pineapple and barbecue sauce and pour over meat. Cook on high heat for 3–4 hours or on low heat 6–8 hours. Serve over rice. *Makes 4–6 servings.*

Serve with broccoli.

EASY CHICKEN BAKE

6	**boneless, skinless chicken breasts**
I can (10 $^3/_4$ ounces)	**cream of mushroom soup**
$^3/_4$ cup	**evaporated milk**
$^1/_4$ teaspoon	**garlic salt**
$^1/_8$ teaspoon	**paprika**
$^1/_4$ cup	**parsley,** fresh chopped, optional

Place chicken in greased 4 to 6-quart slow cooker. Mix together soup, milk, and seasonings. Pour mixture over chicken. Cover and cook on high heat 4 hours or on low heat 8–10 hours. Garnish with fresh chopped parsley, if desired. *Makes 6 servings.*

Serve with brown rice and a side of cooked carrots sprinkled with dill weed.

SUNDAY CHICKEN

4 to 6	**boneless, skinless chicken breasts**
2 cans (10 3/4 ounces each)	**cream of chicken soup**
1 envelope	**dry onion soup mix**
1 cup	**sour cream***

Place chicken in greased 3 1/2 to 5-quart slow cooker. Mix remaining ingredients except sour cream and pour over chicken. Cover and cook on high heat 4 hours or on low heat 6–8 hours. One hour before serving, stir in sour cream. *Makes 4–6 servings.*

Serve with a salad of iceberg lettuce, cauliflower, and radishes.

*May substitute 8 ounces of cream cheese.

78

PINEAPPLE CHICKEN

4 to 6	**boneless, skinless chicken breasts**
$1/8$ teaspoon	**pepper**
	paprika, to taste
1 can (20 ounces)	**pineapple tidbits,** drained
2 tablespoons	**Dijon mustard**
2 to 3 tablespoons	**soy sauce**
$1/4$ teaspoon	**minced garlic**

Place chicken in greased 3 $1/2$ to 5-quart slow cooker. Sprinkle with pepper and paprika. In a separate bowl, mix pineapple, mustard, soy sauce, and garlic together; pour over chicken. Cover and cook on high heat 3–4 hours or on low heat 7–9 hours. *Makes 4–6 servings.*

Serve with oriental vegetables.

LEMONADE CHICKEN

4	**boneless, skinless chicken breasts**
I can (6 ounces)	**frozen lemonade,** thawed
3 tablespoons	**brown sugar**
I tablespoon	**vinegar**
$^1/_4$ cup	**ketchup**

Place chicken in greased 3 to 4 $^1/_2$-quart slow cooker. Stir lemonade concentrate, brown sugar, vinegar, and ketchup together. Mix well. Pour over chicken. Cover and cook on high heat 3–4 hours or on low heat 6–8 hours. *Makes 4 servings.*

Serving suggestion: Thicken the liquid and serve as a sauce for potatoes or rice.

SWEET-AND-SOUR CHICKEN

4 to 6	**boneless, skinless chicken breasts**
1 jar (18 ounces)	**sweet-and-sour sauce**
1 bag (16 ounces)	**frozen Szechuan vegetables stir-fry**
6 cups	**cooked rice**
$^1/_4$ to $^1/_2$ cup	**toasted, chopped almonds,** optional
$^1/_2$ teaspoon	**salt**

Cut chicken into 1-inch pieces. In greased 3 $^1/_2$ to 5-quart slow cooker, combine chicken, sweet-and-sour sauce, frozen vegetables, and salt. Cover and cook on high heat for 2 $^1/_2$–3 hours or on low heat for 5–6 hours. *Makes 4–6 servings.*

Spoon over hot cooked rice and sprinkle with almonds, if desired.

HAWAIIAN HAYSTACKS

10 to 12	**chicken tenders,** cut in chunks
1 cup	**chicken broth**
2 cans (10 3/4 ounces each)	**cream of chicken soup**
1 can (12 ounces)	**evaporated milk**
6 cups	**cooked rice**

Place chicken in greased 3 1/2 to 5-quart slow cooker. Combine remaining ingredients and pour over chicken. Cook on high heat 3–4 hours or on low heat 6–8 hours. *Makes 4–6 servings.*

Serve over hot rice with a variety of cold toppings that could include grated cheese, peas, pineapple tidbits, shredded coconut, raisins, Chinese noodles, olives, diced tomatoes, diced green peppers, sliced green onions, and other family favorites.

CREAMY ITALIAN CHICKEN

4	**frozen boneless, skinless chicken breasts**
I envelope	**dry Italian salad dressing mix**
I can (10 $^3/_4$ ounces)	**cream of chicken soup**

Combine all ingredients in greased 3 $^1/_2$ to 4 $^1/_2$-quart slow cooker. Cover and cook on high heat 6–8 hours or on low heat 10–12 hours. *Makes 4 servings.*

Serve with a salad stack of sliced tomatoes, mozarella cheese, and basil. Top with a favorite dressing.

ITALIAN CHICKEN
WITH MUSHROOMS

4	**boneless, skinless chicken breasts**
I envelope	**Italian salad dressing mix**
$1/4$ cup	**water**
I package (8 ounces)	**cream cheese,** softened
I can (10 $3/4$ ounces)	**cream of chicken soup**
I can (4 ounces)	**mushroom stems and pieces,** drained

Place chicken in greased 3 $1/2$ to 5-quart slow cooker. Combine salad dressing mix and water; pour over chicken. Cover and cook on high heat 3 hours. In a small mixing bowl, beat cream cheese and soup until blended. Stir in mushrooms. Pour over chicken. Cook 2 hours longer on high heat, or until chicken juices run clear. *Makes 4 servings.*

Serve over hot noodles. Accompany with a spinach salad.

CREAMY CHICKEN SOFT TACOS

4	**frozen boneless, skinless chicken breasts**
I jar (16 ounces)	**salsa**
I cup	**sour cream**
6–8	**flour tortillas**

Place chicken in greased 3 $^1/_2$ to 4 $^1/_2$-quart slow cooker. Pour salsa over the top. Cover and cook on high heat 6–8 hours or on low heat 10–12 hours. Shred chicken by pulling apart with two forks. During last hour of cooking, stir in sour cream. *Makes 6–8 servings.*

Fold chicken mix inside warm flour tortillas with lettuce and grated cheddar cheese, if desired.

ORANGE CHICKEN

6	**boneless, skinless chicken breasts**
$1/4$ cup	**molasses**
2 tablespoons	**cider vinegar**
2 tablespoons	**orange juice**
2 tablespoons	**Worcestershire sauce**
2 teaspoons	**Dijon mustard**
$1/8$ to $1/4$ teaspoon	**hot pepper sauce,** optional

Place chicken in greased 4 $1/2$ to 6-quart slow cooker. Combine molasses, vinegar, orange juice, Worcestershire, mustard, and hot sauce if using. Pour sauce over the top of chicken. Cover and cook on high heat 3–4 hours or on low heat 7–9 hours. *Makes 6 servings.*

Serve with white sticky rice and fruit smoothies.

CHICKEN TERIYAKI

10 to 12	**boneless, skinless chicken tenders**
1 bag (16 ounces)	**frozen Oriental vegetables**
1 bottle (18 ounces)	**teriyaki sauce**

Cut chicken tenders in thirds and place in greased 3 to 4 $1/2$-quart slow cooker. Mix frozen vegetables and teriyaki sauce together. Pour over chicken. Cover and cook on high heat 3 hours or on low heat 4–6 hours. *Makes 4–6 servings.*

Serve with rice and fortune cookies.

CHICKEN CACCIATORE

2 to 4	**frozen boneless, skinless chicken breasts**
1 jar (26 ounces)	**chunky vegetable spaghetti sauce**
1/2 teaspoon	**minced garlic**

Place chicken in greased 3 to 4 1/2-quart slow cooker. Pour spaghetti sauce on top of chicken. Sprinkle with minced garlic. Cover and cook on high heat 5–6 hours or on low heat 10–12 hours. *Makes 2–4 servings.*

Serve with a vegetable sauté of zucchini, yellow summer squash, and strips of red pepper.

CHICKEN IN A BAG

I cup	**long-grain converted rice,** uncooked
I can (10 ³/₄ ounces)	**cream of chicken soup**
I ¹/₂ cups	**water**
4 to 6	**boneless, skinless chicken breasts,** cut in bite-size pieces
I envelope	**dry onion soup mix**

Combine rice, cream of chicken soup, and water in greased 3 ¹/₂ to 5-quart slow cooker; stir well.

Place chicken breasts in a see-through roasting bag and add onion soup mix. Shake bag to coat chicken. Puncture 4–6 holes in bottom of bag. Fold top of bag over chicken and place in slow cooker on top of rice mixture. Cover and cook on high heat 4–5 hours or on low heat 8–10 hours. Remove chicken breasts to warm platter. Serve with rice from cooker. *Makes 4–6 servings.*

Serve with potato wedges sprinkled with parmesan cheese.

CHICKEN FAJITAS

4 to 6	**frozen boneless, skinless chicken breasts**
2 ¹/₂ cups	**chunky salsa**
1	**green pepper,** thinly sliced
1	**red pepper,** thinly sliced
¹/₂ cup	**onion,** chopped
1	**large onion,** thinly sliced
	soft flour tortillas*

Place all ingredients in a greased 4 to 6-quart slow cooker. Cover and cook on high heat 5–6 hours or on low heat 10–12 hours. Just before serving, remove fajita mixture with a spoon and shred chicken using two forks.

Place about two rounded tablespoons of chicken mixture in each flour tortilla and top with desired condiments. Fold and roll. *Makes 8–10 servings.*

Condiments for the fajitas can include guacamole, sour cream, grated lettuce, grated cheese, and fresh salsa.

*Pita pockets can be substituted.

CHICKEN PARMESAN

4 to 6	**boneless, skinless chicken breasts**
1 envelope	**dry onion soup mix**
2 cans (10 $^3/_4$ ounces)	**cream of mushroom soup**
1 $^1/_2$ cups	**evaporated milk**
1 cup	**apple juice**
1 cup	**converted white rice,** uncooked
$^1/_4$ teaspoon	**pepper**
$^1/_3$ cup	**grated Parmesan cheese**

Place chicken breasts on the bottom of a greased 3 $^1/_2$ to 5-quart slow cooker. Mix all other ingredients together in a small mixing bowl. Pour soup-and-rice mixture over chicken breasts. Add pepper and sprinkle with grated Parmesan cheese. Cook on high heat 4–6 hours or on low heat 8–10 hours. *Makes 4–6 servings.*

Serve with Caesar salad and crusty bread.

ALMOND CHICKEN

I can (14 ounces)	**chicken broth**
2 strips	**bacon,** cooked and crumbled*
2 tablespoons	**butter**
3 to 4	**boneless, skinless chicken breasts**
1/4 cup	**dried minced onion**
I can (4 ounces)	**sliced mushrooms,** drained
2 tablespoons	**soy sauce**
1/2 teaspoon	**salt**
1 1/2 cups	**celery,** diagonally sliced (optional)
	hot cooked rice
I cup	**toasted slivered almonds****

Combine all ingredients except rice and almonds in greased 3 1/2 to 4 1/2-quart slow cooker. Cover and cook on high heat 3–4 hours or on low heat 6–8 hours. Serve over rice and garnish with almonds. *Makes 4–6 servings.*

Serve with fruit cocktail and almond cookies.

*Do not substitute bacon bits.

**To toast almonds, place them in a single layer on a cookie sheet. Bake at 400 degrees for 4–6 minutes, turning once. The almonds will be golden brown when done.

CHICKEN ENCHILADAS

2 dozen	**corn tortillas**
3 to 4	**boneless, skinless chicken breasts**
I bottle (10 ounces)	**green taco sauce**
$^1/_4$ cup	**dried minced onion**
I can (10 $^3/_4$ ounces)	**cream of mushroom soup**
I can (4 ounces)	**diced green chilies**
2 cups	**grated cheese**
	salt and pepper, to taste

In a greased 3 $^1/_2$ to 4 $^1/_2$-quart slow cooker, layer half of each ingredient in the order listed above. Repeat with second layer. Cover and cook on high heat 30 minutes and then on low heat an additional 3 hours. *Makes 4–6 servings.*

Set out shredded lettuce, diced tomatoes, salsa, and sour cream. Serve with Spanish rice.

COOKED CHICKEN FOR ENTREES, SOUPS, AND STEWS

6 to 8	**boneless, skinless chicken breasts**
2 teaspoons	**garlic powder**
4 cups	**water**
$1/2$ teaspoon	**crushed dried bay leaf**
1 tablespoon	**dried minced onion**

Place all ingredients in 4 $1/2$ to 6-quart slow cooker. Cook on high heat 3–4 hours or on low heat 6–8 hours. Remove chicken from water. Shred or chop chicken to use in casseroles or other dishes. Chicken can be frozen in individual freezer bags for easy use later. *Makes 6–8 servings* of chicken for entrees, soups or stews.

PORK

SAVORY PORK ROAST

4 to 5 pound	**pork loin roast**
$1/2$ cup	**dried minced onion**
2 tablespoons	**soy sauce**
$1/4$ teaspoon	**crushed dried bay leaf**
1 tablespoon	**garlic powder**

Place roast and onion in greased 4 $1/2$ to 5-quart slow cooker. Add soy sauce, bay leaf, and garlic powder. Cover and cook on low heat 7−9 hours. *Makes 8−10 servings.*

Serve with mashed potatoes and broccoli.

CRANBERRY PORK ROAST

2 1/2 to 3 pounds	**boneless, rolled pork loin**
1/2 teaspoon	**salt**
1/4 teaspoon	**pepper**
1 can (16 ounces)	**whole berry cranberry sauce***
1/4 cup	**honey**
1 teaspoon	**fresh grated orange peel**
1/8 teaspoon	**ground cloves**
1/8 teaspoon	**ground nutmeg**

Place roast in greased 4 1/2 to 6-quart slow cooker. Sprinkle with salt and pepper. Combine the remaining ingredients; pour over roast. Cover and cook on low heat 4–5 hours, or until a meat thermometer reads 165 degrees. For extra-tender meat, cook an additional 2 hours. Let stand 10 minutes before slicing. *Makes 4–6 servings.*

Serve with garlic mashed potatoes and rolls.

*Do not use jellied cranberry sauce as it adds too much liquid.

BARBECUED PORK CHOPS

6	**pork chops**
I bottle (16 ounces)	**barbecue sauce**

Brush each pork chop with sauce and then place in greased 3 $^{1}/_{2}$ to 5-quart slow cooker and pour remaining sauce over top. Cover and cook on low heat 7–8 hours. *Makes 6 servings.*

Serve with your favorite potato salad.

ITALIAN PORK CHOPS

6 **pork chops**
1 bottle (16 ounces) **Italian salad dressing**

Place pork chops in greased 3 $^1/_2$ to 5-quart slow cooker and pour salad dressing over top. Cover and cook on high heat 6–8 hours or on low heat 10–12 hours. *Makes 6 servings.*

Serve with couscous or brown rice.

SWEET-AND-SOUR PORK

1 pound	**pork tenderloin,** cut into 1-inch pieces
1 can (20 ounces)	**pineapple chunks,** drained
1 cup	**sweet-and-sour sauce**
1/4 teaspoon	**ground ginger**

Place all ingredients in the order listed above in greased 2 to 3 1/2-quart slow cooker. Cover and cook on low heat 4–6 hours. *Makes 2–4 servings.*

Spoon over hot cooked rice and serve steamed oriental vegetables on the side.

POLYNESIAN PORK CHOPS

4 to 6 **lean pork chops**
I can (8 ounces) **crushed pineapple**
I cup **barbecue sauce**

Place pork chops in greased 3 $\frac{1}{2}$ to 5-quart slow cooker. Combine pineapple and barbecue sauce, and pour over meat. Cook on high heat 3–4 hours or on low heat 6–8 hours. *Makes 4–6 servings.*

Serve with buttered sweet potatoes.

PORK CHOPS AND MUSHROOMS

4	**boneless pork chops,** $1/2$-inch thick
2	**medium onions,** sliced
I can (4 ounces)	**sliced mushrooms,** drained
I envelope	**dry onion soup mix**
$1/2$ cup	**water**
I can (10 $3/4$ ounces)	**cream of mushroom soup**

Place meat in greased 3 $1/2$ to 4 $1/2$-quart slow cooker. Top with onions and mushrooms. In a separate bowl, combine soup mix, water, and soup. Pour over mushrooms and pork chops. Cover and cook on low heat 6–8 hours. *Makes 4 servings.*

Serve with baked potatoes.

PORK CHOP CASSEROLE

4 to 6	**pork chops**
3 cups	**water**
1 cup	**long-grain converted rice,** uncooked
1 can (10 3/4 ounces)	**cream of mushroom soup**
1 teaspoon	**salt**
1 teaspoon	**dried parsley**
1/4 teaspoon	**pepper**

Place pork chops in greased 3 1/2 to 5-quart slow cooker. Combine remaining ingredients and pour over pork chops. Cover and cook on high heat 3–4 hours or on low heat 6–8 hours. *Makes 4–6 servings.*

Serve with a salad of leaf lettuce, berries, and crumbled blue cheese.

EHLERS' PORK RIBS

3 to 4 pounds	**boneless pork ribs**
1	**onion,** sliced
2 cups	**barbecue sauce**
2 teaspoons	**lemon juice**

Combine all ingredients in greased 3 $^1/_2$ to 5-quart slow cooker. Cover and cook on low heat 8–10 hours. *Makes 4–6 servings.*

Serve with with macaroni salad, baked beans, and potato chips.

*This recipe can be easily doubled to fit a 6 to 7-quart slow cooker.

BARBECUE PORK SANDWICHES

2 to 3 pounds	**boneless pork roast**
$^3/_4$ cup	**dried minced onion**
1 bottle (12 ounces)	**barbecue sauce**
$^1/_4$ cup	**honey**
	sandwich rolls

Place roast in greased 3 $^1/_2$ to 5-quart slow cooker. Combine onion, barbecue sauce, and honey. Pour mixture over meat. Cover and cook on low heat 6–8 hours. When roast is done, use two forks to shred meat. *Makes 4–6 servings.*

Offer a variety of sandwich rolls with coleslaw on the side.

SHREDDED PORK BURRITOS

3 1/2 pounds **boneless pork loin roast**
1 teaspoon **salt**
1/2 teaspoon **pepper**
1 1/2 teaspoons **minced garlic**
1 cup **water**
4 to 6 **warm flour tortillas***

Place pork roast in greased 4 to 5-quart slow cooker. Sprinkle salt, pepper, and minced garlic over the top of roast. Add water. Cover and cook on low heat 8–9 hours, or until pork is tender.

With a slotted spoon, remove pork from slow cooker and discard the liquid. Shred meat with two forks and use as burrito filling. *Makes 4–6 servings.*

Set out bowls of lettuce, cheese, and diced tomatoes for toppings.

*To make tacos, substitute flour tortillas for corn taco shells.

PORK SAUSAGE CASSEROLE

1 pound	**bulk sausage**
1 envelope	**dry chicken soup mix**
1 cup	**long-grain converted rice,** uncooked
2	**stalks celery,** diced
1/3 cup	**slivered almonds**
4 cups	**water**
1/2 teaspoon	**salt**

Combine all ingredients in greased 3 1/2 to 5-quart slow cooker and stir well. Cover and cook on high heat for 3–4 hours or on low heat for 7–9 hours, until rice is tender. *Makes 2–4 servings.*

Serve with a fresh sauté of swiss chard or baby spinach, red onion, and crumbled bacon. Season with Balsamic vinegar.

HAM AND POTATOES

1 package (32 ounces)	**frozen hashed brown potatoes**
1 teaspoon	**salt**
1/2 teaspoon	**pepper**
1 can (10 3/4 ounces)	**cream of chicken soup**
1 can (12 ounces)	**evaporated milk**
1 1/2 cups	**cooked ham,** chopped
2 cups	**grated cheddar cheese,** divided

Mix all ingredients except one cup cheddar cheese in greased 3 1/2 to 5-quart slow cooker. Cover and cook on low heat 5–6 hours. Thirty minutes before serving, sprinkle reserved cheddar cheese over the top. *Makes 4–6 servings.*

Serve with cold green beans and red pepper with vinaigrette dressing.

RED POTATOES WITH HAM

2 pounds	**red potatoes,** quartered or halved
2 cups	**cooked ham,** chopped or diced
I can (10 3/4 ounces)	**cream of potato soup**
1/2 to 1 envelope	**dry Ranch salad dressing mix**
8 ounces	**cream cheese,** softened*

Place potatoes and ham in greased 3 1/2 to 5-quart slow cooker. Beat together soup and salad dressing mix. Stir into potatoes and ham. Cover and cook on low heat 8 hours. Add the cream cheese during the last hour of cooking. Stir before serving. *Makes 2–4 servings.*

Serve with steamed carrots, cauliflower and broccoli. Pass crusty bread.

*Light cream cheese may be substituted.

HOLIDAY HAM

3 to 5 pound	**ham**
24 to 36	**whole cloves**
1/2 cup	**pineapple juice**
1/4 cup	**honey**

Pierce ham with cloves; cover entire ham. Place in a greased 4 to 6-quart slow cooker. Pour juice and honey over ham. Cover and cook on low heat 6–9 hours. Remove cloves before slicing and serving. *Makes 8–10 servings.*

Accompany with a salad of red cabbage, celery, and carrot.

SHREDDED HAM SANDWICHES

2 pounds	**shredded ham**
1 bottle (20 ounces)	**cola***
1 bottle (16 ounces)	**barbecue sauce**
	hamburger buns

Combine all ingredients in greased 3 $\frac{1}{2}$ to 5-quart slow cooker. Cover and cook on high heat 4–5 hours or on low heat 8–10 hours. Using a slotted spoon, remove ham and serve on hamburger buns. *Makes 4–6 servings.*

Serve with potato salad.

*Do not substitute diet cola.

DESSERTS

CARROT CAKE

1 1/2 cups	**flour**
3/4 cup	**sugar**
2	**large eggs**
1/4 cup	**water**
1/3 cup	**vegetable oil**
1 teaspoon	**baking powder**
1/2 teaspoon	**baking soda**
3/4 teaspoon	**cinnamon**
1/4 teaspoon	**nutmeg**
1 cup	**grated carrots**

Combine all ingredients in a 2-quart mixing bowl by hand. Spread batter in greased 2 to 3 1/2-quart slow cooker. Cover and cook on low heat for 2 hours, or until firm in the center. (You can lightly jiggle the covered slow cooker to check firmness.) *Makes 4–6 servings.*

Top with whipped topping or your favorite cream cheese frosting.

CARAMEL ROLLS

2 packages (8 ounces each) **refrigerator biscuits**
$^1/_4$ cup **melted butter**
$^1/_2$ cup **brown sugar**
$^1/_2$ teaspoon **cinnamon**

Mix sugar and cinnamon together in small bowl. Dip individual biscuits into melted butter and then into cinnamon and sugar mixture. Place each covered biscuit in greased 3 $^1/_2$ to 5-quart slow cooker. Cook on high heat 2 $^1/_2$–3 hours, or until rolls are done. You can check rolls in the center after 2 hours for doneness. *Makes 6–8 servings.*

TRIPLE RICH CHOCOLATE CAKE

1 box (18 ounces)	**devil's food cake mix**
4	**eggs**
1 cup	**light sour cream**
$^3/_4$ cup	**vegetable oil**
1 cup	**water**
1 package (3 ounces)	**instant chocolate pudding**
1 cup	**chocolate chips**

Combine all ingredients by hand in a 2-quart mixing bowl.* Pour batter into greased 3 $^1/_2$ to 5-quart slow cooker. Cover and cook on low heat 5–6 hours, or until done in the center. Do not cook this recipe on high heat. *Makes 8–10 servings.*

*It is important that you combine ingredients by hand and not with a mixer.

SUGAR AND SPICE CAKE

1 box (18 ounces)	**yellow cake mix**
4	**eggs**
1 cup	**light sour cream**
3/4 cup	**vegetable oil**
1 cup	**water**
1 package (3 ounces)	**instant vanilla pudding**
1/4 cup	**sugar**
1 teaspoon	**cinnamon**

Combine all ingredients except cinnamon and sugar by hand in a 2-quart mixing bowl; set aside.* Combine cinnamon and sugar together in a small bowl. Sprinkle cinnamon-sugar mixture in greased 3 1/2 to 5-quart slow cooker, making sure to cover the bottom and sides. Spread batter in slow cooker. Cover and cook on low heat 5–6 hours, or until done in the center. Do not cook this recipe on high heat. *Makes 8–10 servings.*

*It is important that you combine ingredients by hand and not with a mixer.

CHERRY BISCUIT COBBLER

2 packages (8 ounces each)	**refrigerator biscuits,** separated and quartered
I can (21 ounces)	**cherry pie filling**
$1/3$ cup	**brown sugar**
$1/2$ teaspoon	**cinnamon**
$1/3$ cup	**melted butter** or **margarine**

Mix together brown sugar, cinnamon, and melted butter in a small bowl. Mixture will be lumpy. Grease a 3 $1/2$ to 5-quart slow cooker, then layer I package biscuits, half the cinnamon-and-sugar mixture, and then half the pie filling. Add the second package of biscuits; cover with the remaining half of the cinnamon-and-sugar mixture, and top with the remaining half of the pie filling. Cover and cook on high heat 2 $1/2$–3 hours, or until biscuits are done in the center. *Makes 6–8 servings.*

EASY GRANOLA APPLE CRISP

2 cans (21 ounces each)	**apple pie filling**
2 ¹/₂ cups	**granola cereal**
1 ¹/₂ teaspoons	**cinnamon**
¹/₃ cup	**sugar**
¹/₃ cup	**melted butter** or **margarine**

Place pie filling on bottom of greased 3 to 4 ¹/₂-quart slow cooker. In the order listed above, sprinkle remaining ingredients over the pie filling. Cover and cook on low heat 3 hours. *Makes 6–8 servings.*

Serve warm with vanilla ice cream or whipped topping.

CHERRY JUBILEE

2 cans (21 ounces each)	**cherry pie filling**
1 package (18 ounces)	**yellow cake mix**
$^1/_2$ cup	**melted butter** or **margarine**

Spread pie filling in the bottom of greased 4 $^1/_2$ to 6-quart slow cooker. Sprinkle dry cake mix powder over the top. Pour melted butter over the top. Cover and cook on high heat 2 hours or on low heat 4 hours. *Makes 10–12 servings.*

Serve with vanilla ice cream or whipped topping.

LEMON CUSTARD CAKE

Batter:

1 package (13.9 oz)	lemon–poppy seed quick bread mix
1	egg
1 cup	light sour cream
$^1/_2$ cup	water

Sauce:

1 tablespoon	vegetable oil
$^3/_4$ cup	water
$^1/_2$ cup	sugar
$^1/_4$ cup	freshly squeezed lemon juice

Mix batter ingredients by hand in 2-quart mixing bowl. Pour batter in greased 3 $^1/_2$ to 4-quart slow cooker. Mix sauce ingredients together in separate bowl. Pour sauce evenly over batter. Do not stir after sauce has been added. Cover and cook on high heat 2–2 $^1/_2$ hours. Allow cake to cool for 30 minutes before serving.

Makes 6–8 servings.

PINEAPPLE UPSIDE-DOWN CAKE

I box (18 ounces)	**yellow cake mix**
¼ cup	**melted butter**
⅛ cup	**brown sugar**
I can (15 ounces)	**crushed pineapple,** with liquid
8 to 12	**maraschino cherries,** halved

In a 2-quart mixing bowl, make cake batter according to the directions on back of box. In a greased 3 ½ to 5-quart slow cooker, layer melted butter, brown sugar, pineapple with juice, and cherries. Pour cake batter over the top. Cover and cook on low heat 4–5 hours, or until cake is firm in the center. *Makes 8–10 servings.*

CHOCOLATE CUSTARD CAKE

Batter:

2 cups of a packaged	**brownie mix**
1	**large egg**
1 tablespoon	**vegetable oil**
$^1/_4$ cup	**water**

Sauce:

1 cup	**hot water**
$^1/_2$ cup	**brown sugar**
3 tablespoons	**baking cocoa**

In a 2-quart mixing bowl, mix batter ingredients by hand. Pour batter in greased 3 $^1/_2$ to 4-quart slow cooker. Mix sauce ingredients together in separate bowl. Pour sauce evenly over batter. Do not stir after sauce has been added. Cover and cook on high heat 2–2 $^1/_2$ hours. Allow cake to cool for 30 minutes before serving. Serve with vanilla ice cream. *Makes 6–8 servings.*

NOTES

NOTES

ABOUT THE AUTHORS

Stephanie Ashcraft was raised near Kirklin, Indiana. She received a bachelor's degree in family science and a teaching certificate from Brigham Young University. Stephanie loves teaching, interacting with people, and spending time with friends and family. Since 1998, she has taught cooking classes for Macey's Little Cooking Theater in Provo and Orem, Utah. She and her husband, Ivan, reside in Provo with their children. Being a mom is her full-time job.

Janet Eyring was raised in Utah. She received a bachelor's degree in recreation management and youth leadership from Brigham Young University. Janet loves spending time with friends and family and enjoys time away from her kitchen. Since 2000, she has taught a monthly cooking class, Slow-Cooker Sensations, for Macey's Little Cooking Theater in Pleasant Grove, Orem, and Provo, Utah, where she met Stephanie. She and her husband Shawn reside in Heber, Utah, with their children.